A science CHAPTER BOOK

The Magic School Bus®

CHAPTER BOOK

VOYAGE TO THE VOLCANO

The Magic School Bus® CHAPTER BOOK

VOYAGE TO THE VOLCANO

SCHOLASTIC INC.
New York   Toronto   London   Auckland   Sydney
Mexico City   New Delhi   Hong Kong   Buenos Aires

Written by Judith Stamper.

Illustrations by John Speirs.

Based on *The Magic School Bus* books
written by Joanna Cole and illustrated by Bruce Degen.

No part of this publication may be reproduced in whole or in part, or stored in a retrieval system, or transmitted in any form or by any means, electronic, mechanical, photocopying, recording, or otherwise, without written permission of the publisher. For information regarding permission, write to Scholastic Inc., Attention: Permissions Department, 557 Broadway, New York, NY 10012.

ISBN 0-439-42935-8

25 24 23 22 21 20 19   7 8/0

Designed by Peter Koblish

Printed in the U.S.A.   40

The author and editor would like to thank
Professor Ken Rubin of the Hawaii Center for Volcanology
for his expert advice in reviewing this manuscript.

INTRODUCTION.

Hi, my name is Dorothy Ann (D.A. for short). I am one of the kids in Ms. Frizzle's class.

You've probably heard of Ms. Frizzle. (Sometimes we just call her the Friz.) She is a terrific teacher, but a little strange.

Ms. Frizzle loves science and will do anything to teach us about it. That's why the Magic School Bus comes in handy. Believe me, it's not called *magic* for nothing. Once we climb on board, *anything* can happen!

We can usually tell when a Magic School Bus trip is coming up. How? We just look at what Ms. Frizzle is wearing.

One day, the Friz came into class wearing an orange dress with erupting volcanoes all over it. Since we were studying volcanoes, I didn't get suspicious right away.

But it didn't take long for Ms. Frizzle to find an excuse to take a field trip. And before we knew it, we were piling on board the Magic School Bus to go on a mysterious trip to the land of volcanoes.

Let me tell you what happened when the Magic School Bus got caught in a hot spot in the Ring of Fire!

CHAPTER 1

"Dorothy Ann, Tim, are your teams ready for the next question?" Ms. Frizzle asked.

We were in the middle of a class quiz bowl about volcanoes. My team was competing against Tim's team — and the competition was as red-hot as molten lava.

I shot a quick glance at my quiz bowl teammates — Carlos, Phoebe, and Ralphie. They all gave me a thumbs-up.

"Ready, Ms. Frizzle," I said confidently.

"Ready, Ms. Frizzle," Tim said, just as confidently.

Ms. Frizzle reached her hand into the bowlful of questions she had prepared for the

1

volcano quiz bowl. As she pulled one out, I looked at the scoreboard.

DOROTHY ANN'S TEAM: 7 POINTS

TIM'S TEAM: 7 POINTS

Unbelievable! I knew everything there was to know about volcanoes. I had crammed my head full of facts and figures for weeks. I had drilled Carlos, Phoebe, and Ralphie about everything we knew. But somehow Tim and his team had kept up with us!

My finger was itching to press the buzzer as Ms. Frizzle unfolded the question and read it.

The Friz cleared her throat. "What big volcano erupted in the United States in 1980?"

Blaaaahhht! My buzzer was the first to go off!

"Dorothy Ann, what's your answer?" the Friz asked.

"Mount Saint Helens erupted in 1980 in Washington State," I said. "According to my research, the eruption blew the top right off the mountain."

Mount Saint Helens Blows Its Top!
by D.A.

When Mount Saint Helens blew its top, it sent hot ash and glowing gas 12 miles (19 km) into the air! The eruption lasted for nine hours and was heard more than 200 miles (322 km) away.

Before it blew up, Mount Saint Helens was a popular vacation spot. It hadn't erupted since 1857!

"Correct," the Friz said. "That makes the score eight to seven, with Dorothy Ann's team in the lead."

Yes! I gave Phoebe a high five.

"Hands on your buzzers, teams," Ms. Frizzle said. "Here's the next question."

As we waited for the Friz to read out the next question, I quickly ran through the names of the top ten volcanic eruptions in the history of the world, just in case.

"This is a tough one," Ms. Frizzle said. "Where is the farthest away that volcanoes have been found?"

My mind drew a blank. In desperation, I looked at Phoebe, Carlos, and Ralphie. Their faces were blanks, too.

Blaaahhtt! Tim's buzzer sounded off like a fire alarm.

"Tim," Ms. Frizzle said. "What is your answer?"

"There are volcanoes in outer space," Tim said with a smile. "That's as far from us as you can get."

"Out of this world, Tim," Ms. Frizzle said. "Your team gets another point. The score stands at eight to eight."

"Wow, Tim," I said with admiration. "How did you know that?"

"I read about it once in a science fiction story," Tim said. "And I'm writing a report on it."

Out-of-This-World Eruptions
by Tim

Earth isn't the only planet with volcanoes. Scientists believe that Venus still has active volcanoes. And one of Jupiter's moons, Io, has eight volcanoes. One theory is that Jupiter's rings are actually made up of dust from Io's volcanoes!

"Next question," the Friz announced.

I looked down the row of my teammates. Carlos was missing! How had he managed to sneak away? And where was he?

We found out a second later. There was a funny bubbling noise from the back of the room. We all looked over to where Arnold's model volcano stood. Something red was starting to flow from its top!

"My volcano," Arnold screamed. "It's erupting!"

The volcano began to spit out red liquid all over the room. Carlos suddenly stood up from behind the model. His face was covered with splotches of fake lava.

"Carlos, did you pour vinegar into my volcano?" Arnold demanded.

"Is that what this is?" Carlos asked, holding up a plastic bottle.

"Oh, no," Ms. Frizzle said. "We've got to get that thing out of here before it blows its top all over the room!"

The Friz rushed to pick up the model volcano that had lava flowing down its sides and onto the floor. She carried it out the class-room door and set it on the ground outside. Some lava flowed out onto the Friz. But it

blended right in with the orange lava bursting out of the volcanoes on her dress.

Ms. Frizzle came back inside and we all rushed to the window to watch the volcanic action.

"It looks just like a *real* volcano!" Phoebe said.

"But *I* wanted to make it explode," Arnold said with a sniffle.

"Why don't you tell us how your model works?" Ms. Frizzle said. "And later, you can make it erupt again."

Ready, Set, Blow!
by Arnold

Just follow these simple steps to make your own model volcano.
1. Put about 4 tablespoons of baking soda in a bottle. You can put the bottle inside a model volcano made of modeling clay or papier-mâché.

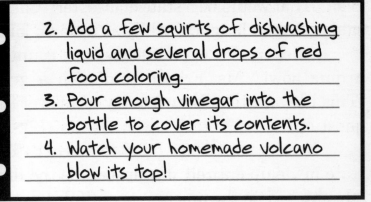

> 2. Add a few squirts of dishwashing liquid and several drops of red food coloring.
> 3. Pour enough vinegar into the bottle to cover its contents.
> 4. Watch your homemade volcano blow its top!

"Ms. Frizzle, can we get back to the quiz bowl?" Tim asked.

I rushed to my seat and put my hand over the buzzer. "I'm ready," I announced.

Everyone else took his or her seat, and the Friz dipped into the quiz bowl for another question.

"What state is made up entirely of volcanoes?" Ms. Frizzle asked.

Just as I was ready to push down on my buzzer, I saw Carlos's hand reach over and press it.

Blaaahhht!

"Carlos, what's the answer?" Ms. Frizzle asked.

9

"That would be a state of disaster!" Carlos said and then laughed wildly at his own joke.

"Nice try, Carlos, but jokes don't count in a quiz bowl," Ms. Frizzle said with a grin. "Tim, it's your team's turn to try to answer the question."

Keesha raised her hand to answer. "The state made up entirely of volcanoes is the fiftieth state to join the union — beautiful Hawaii!"

A State of Volcanoes
by Keesha

The Hawaiian Islands were formed over a hot spot in the middle of the Pacific Ocean. Underwater volcanoes erupted from the hot spot and grew high enough to form islands. At first, there was only one Hawaiian island. But over many millions of years, the entire chain of islands was formed.

"Right you are!" Ms. Frizzle said with a smile. "Hawaii is a hot spot for volcanoes!"

I was feeling a little hot myself. The score was now nine to eight in favor of Tim's team. Whichever team got to 10 first was the winner. I wiped my hand across my sweating forehead and got ready for the next question.

Ms. Friz pulled the question out of the bowl. "What do you call lava when it's still inside a volcano?"

From Magma to Lava
by D.A.

The earth's interior is much hotter than the surface, so hot that in some places, it melts rocks. This melted rock becomes a thick, gooey, pasty substance called magma. When magma erupts from a volcano and hits the air, it becomes lava. Lava is a red-hot liquid that later cools and becomes solid rock.

It only took me three seconds to hit that buzzer. *Blaaahhht!*

"D.A., what is your answer?" the Friz asked.

"Magma," I said loudly and clearly. "While it's still inside a volcano, lava is called magma."

"Score one for Dorothy Ann's team," Ms. Frizzle said. "It looks like it's all tied up again at nine to nine. And here is the tiebreaker question."

Tim and I eyed each other across the room. We waited as the Friz pulled out the question and read it.

"What is the most active volcano on Earth today?" Ms. Frizzle asked.

The room was filled with a dead silence. I fiddled with my pencil as I racked my brain for the answer. I looked at Carlos, Phoebe, and Ralphie. They just shrugged their shoulders. I looked at Tim. He was scratching his head. Ms. Frizzle had stumped all of us!

Ms. Frizzle got up and wiped a blob of red lava off her dress. Then she reached over and picked up Liz off her desk.

"Liz, I think it's time for a field trip. Do you want to go see a volcano erupt?"

Liz let out a squeak and the rest of us — except Arnold, of course — erupted into a cheer.

"I knew I should have stayed home today," Arnold said with a sigh.

"Follow me," the Friz said as she headed toward the door. "We're going on a mystery trip to the most active volcano on Earth — and the first team to figure out where we're going wins the quiz bowl!"

Tim and I grabbed our buzzers. Then we sprinted neck and neck to the Magic School Bus. We both wanted the best view out the window of the bus.

I knew right then that this wasn't going to be any ordinary field trip. It was going to be a duel of brains and brawn — and may the best kid win!

I reached the door of the Magic School Bus first, ran up the steps, and slid into the window seat, right behind Ms. Frizzle.

I was ready to roll!

CHAPTER 2

Tim slid into the seat beside me. Then he leaned forward to check out the Magic School Bus's instrument panel. Ms. Frizzle was busy fiddling with the dials as the rest of the kids boarded the bus.

"Okay, kids," the Friz announced, "prepare for takeoff. We're in for a long flight!"

"A long flight?" Tim said. "Does that mean we're crossing an ocean?"

"That's correct, Tim!" Ms. Frizzle said.

"So that rules out Mount Saint Helens," I said.

"And Paricutín in Mexico," Tim added.

"Right," I said, impressed that Tim knew

14

that. I began to worry that I might be slipping as the science whiz of Ms. Frizzle's class. I made up my mind right then and there to read five more encyclopedia entries a day!

Ms. Frizzle started up the Magic School Bus and rolled out of the parking lot. When she pressed the red button with a jet on it, I knew it wouldn't be long before we were airborne.

Outside my window, I saw the Magic School Bus sprout wings. The jet engines started to roar, and soon we were streaking down the road — I mean, runway — and lifting off.

"Wahoo," Carlos yelled. "We're out of here!"

"Please tell us where we're going, Ms. Frizzle," Arnold pleaded. "I don't like surprises."

"Don't worry, Arnold," the Friz said. "You'll love this surprise!"

Tim glanced at me with a puzzled look on his face. Where could we be going that Arnold would like? Arnold didn't like any surprises!

"Maybe we're going someplace cool," Tim said.

"Or someplace hot," I added.

"Oh, no," Tim said. "She wouldn't take us *inside* a volcano, would she?"

We both stared at the back of the Friz's head in front of us. Her curly red hair was standing on end with excitement. Who knew *what* we were in for!

Soon, the Magic School Jet had gained enough altitude to be up above the clouds. Every few minutes, Tim and I looked out the window to see if we could tell where we were going. But all we could see were fluffy white clouds.

Those clouds must have looked like sheep, because I fell asleep while counting them. I don't know how long I was sleeping, but I woke up with a start when Keesha started to shriek.

"Look," she yelled. "Down below us. It's Hawaii!"

I was still half asleep, but I knew I had to grab for my buzzer. I found it just in time.

Blaaahhhttt! Blaaahhht!

Tim's buzzer went off at exactly the same time as mine.

"Kilauea!" we both yelled.

"Correct!" Ms. Frizzle said with a giggle. "You both came up with the right answer. Kilauea, on the big island of Hawaii, is the most active volcano in the world. And it looks like we still need a tiebreaker in the quiz bowl."

Tim and I looked at each other. This was getting tough!

"Listen up," the Friz said. "Here's the next tiebreaker question. . . . What is the Hawaiian name for smooth, flat lava?"

I searched every corner of my brain. And I came up with — nothing! I looked over at Tim. He looked as clueless as I did.

"Carlos, do you know the answer to that?" I asked hopefully.

"Hmmm," Carlos said. "Smooth and flat . . . Could it be a sidewalk?"

"I'm afraid not, Carlos," the Friz said with a smile. "Looks like all of you have something to learn while we're in Hawaii!"

Down below us, the islands of Hawaii looked like green jigsaw puzzle pieces on the blue ocean. Carlos began to count them.

How Many Hawaiian Islands?
by Carlos

Hawaii is made up of about 132 islands, making a chain about 2,500 miles (4,023 km) long! There are eight main islands, and most people live on seven of these eight islands.

Hawaiian Islands:

Hawaii	Molokai
Maui	Oahu
Kahoolawe	Kauai
Lanai	Niihau

"Did all those islands really start out as volcanoes?" Phoebe asked.

But for once, Ms. Frizzle was too busy to answer her. She seemed to be having a problem with the Magic School Jet. I saw her press the landing gear button over and over again. It wasn't working!

"Uh, kids," the Friz said in a nervous voice. "We're experiencing some technical difficulties. The landing gear seems to be stuck. That means we have to PREPARE FOR AN EMERGENCY LANDING!"

The Friz said that last part in a voice that meant business! Life preservers popped out of the overhead compartments into our laps. We jumped up and strapped them on.

"Okay," the Friz announced. "This is a new trick for the Magic School Bus, but I think it will work out okay."

"You *think* it will work out!" Arnold yelled in a hysterical voice.

"Trust me, Arnold," the Friz said. "And grab hold of the sides of the raft!"

Tim and I looked at each other again. Raft? What raft? A second later, we found out.

The Magic School Jet turned into a big yellow raft in midair! Soon we were falling down out of the sky, grabbing hold of the sides of the raft like our lives depended on it. And they did!

I peeked over the side of the raft as we were flying down through the air. Below us was the blue water of the Pacific Ocean. It looked scary — but not as scary as green land would have looked!

"Hold on tight!" the Friz yelled. "We're about to land — NOW!"

KERSPLASH!

Our yellow raft hit the top of a huge ocean wave. I could feel the spray of salt water on my face. Then I felt my stomach flop around like a fish. We were riding the wave in our raft — like a gigantic surfboard!

"Awesome!" Carlos yelled.

"Surf's up!" Arnold screamed.

The surf was up, all right! Our wave was

From the Desk of Ms. Frizzle

Surf's Up!

Surfing has been around for a long time. People in Hawaii were surfing before Christopher Columbus landed in the Americas in 1492.

To catch a wave, a surfer lies face-down on a surfboard and paddles out to where the waves begin. When a wave grows about 3 feet (91 cm) tall, the surfer stands up on the board. Then she rides the wave into the shore.

at least 10 feet higher than the surface of the ocean in front of us. And we were coming into shore fast!

All of a sudden, the big wave hit the bottom of the ocean floor close to the shore. A second later, we spilled out of the raft into the shallow water along the beach. The Magic School Raft floated up onto the sand nearby.

"Welcome to Hawaii, class," Ms. Frizzle said with a grin.

"Uh, Ms. Frizzle," Arnold said. "I think we may have landed in outer space. There's something very weird about this sand."

We all looked down at the sand under our feet. It was black. We stumbled out of the water onto the beach. The sand there was black, too.

"I can tell you've never been to Hawaii before, Arnold," said Ms. Frizzle. "This sand isn't weird at all."

"Hey, this would make a strange sand castle," Carlos said, starting to dig in the sand.

"I know why the sand is black," Wanda said. "It's all because of volcanoes."

"Wow, check out that surfer dude," Carlos suddenly yelled, pointing toward the water.

Black Beaches
by Wanda

Islands with volcanoes, like Hawaii and Iceland, have beaches with black sand. Black sand is created when hot lava meets the cool ocean. The lava is shattered into small particles that make the sand.

So why is the sand black? It is black because of all the dark minerals, like iron, that are in the lava.

We looked out at the ocean and saw a surfer coming in on a big wave. He had on wild Hawaiian-print shorts and was riding his surfboard like a pro. He rode the wave right onto the shore where we stood.

"Hey," he said with an amazed look on his face. "Did you guys just fall out of the sky on a raft?"

Ms. Frizzle walked over to the big yellow raft and pulled the plug on its air supply. There was a sudden blast of air that made the black sand swirl up around the raft. We couldn't see a thing for a minute, then the air cleared. Standing on the beach was the Magic School Bus!

"Ms. Frizzle, I presume?" the surfer asked in surprise.

"The one and only," the Friz said with a smile.

"I've heard all about you," the surfer

said. "My cousin who lives on the mainland used to be one of your students! I'm Jim Russell. I'm a volcanologist at Volcanoes National Park."

"Nice to meet you, Jim," the Friz said, shaking his hand.

"You're a volca-what?" Arnold asked.

"I'm a volcanologist," Jim said. "I study volcanoes."

From Jim's Volcanologist Files

A Hot Job

A volcanologist is a scientist who studies volcanoes. On the job, a volcanologist collects lava, gas samples, and other data to try to predict when a new eruption might happen.

A volcanologist gets into a lot of hot spots — you have to think fast to outsmart a volcano!

"Would you like to come with us to see Kilauea?" I asked. I had a secret plan all ready. I would get Jim alone and ask him about the Hawaiian name for smooth, flat lava.

Just then, Tim broke into our conversation.

"Hey, Jim, do you know the Hawaiian name for smooth, flat lava?" Tim asked.

"The answer is somewhere in Volcanoes National Park," Jim said. "That's all I will tell you. Can I hitch a ride in the Magic School Bus back to my house? I've got to pick up my volcanologist gear — and then we'll go see Kilauea!"

"Excellent!" we all yelled as we piled into the bus.

The Friz slipped in behind the wheel. As she started the bus, its wheels spun up some black sand. Then we were off . . . ready to explore the red-hot heart of the most active volcano on Earth!

CHAPTER 3

Jim sat next to me on the Magic School Bus after he picked up his volcanologist gear. He told me I could look through his pack. It was full of clothes and instruments.

"Hey, why do you have an astronaut suit in here?" I asked.

"It's not exactly a space suit," Jim said. "But it is made for some pretty alien conditions. When you're down inside a volcano, you never know what might happen. The temperature could heat up, or poisonous gas could spurt out, or a chunk of lava could fly at you. That suit helps protect us."

"Whoa!" Carlos suddenly yelled, pointing outside the window. "I think I see some lava. Are we getting close to the volcano?"

"You bet we are," Jim said. "That lava you just saw is only a year old. It oozed right over a stand of trees that used to be here."

"How long has Kilauea been pumping out lava?" Ralphie asked.

"This latest eruption started in 1983, when I was just a little kid," Jim said. "I remember my mom and dad yelling at me to wake up and look at the sky. I ran outside, and it looked like the sky was on fire. Kilauea was erupting . . . and it hasn't stopped since!"

KILAUEA VOLCANO
ERUPTION 1983

From Jim's Volcanologist Files

Kilauea Fast Facts

- Kilauea is the world's most active volcano.
- The Kilauea volcano is in Hawaii Volcanoes National Park.
- Kilauea's crater is 2½ miles (4 km) long, 2 miles (3.2 km) wide, and 400 feet (122 m) deep.
- Kilauea last began erupting in 1983 and continues to burn today. It is the longest-lived eruption in Hawaiian volcano history. This particular eruption is called Puu Oo.
- Every minute, 350,000 to 8,000,000 gallons (1,325,000–30,280,000 l) of molten rock ooze from Kilauea. That's enough molten rock to cover all 63 square miles (163 sq km) of Washington, D.C., in just five days!
- Kilauea has set more than 16,000 acres (64.8 sq km) of lowland and rain forest on fire, destroying the habitats of several endangered species.
- Every day, the volcano spits out more than 2,500 tons of sulfur dioxide, enough gas to fill 100 blimps!

"But how can we visit it if it's erupting?" Arnold asked. "Won't we get covered in lava?"

"Not if you're careful and obey the signs," Jim said. "Kilauea is a slow and steady kind of volcano."

A few minutes later, we passed the entrance to Volcanoes National Park. Compared to most national parks, it's pretty wild. It may not have bears and deer, but it does have real live volcanoes!

"Ms. Frizzle," Jim asked, "could you drop me off at the park headquarters? I'm going to meet up with another volcanologist. We're taking measurements of the air quality inside the Kilauea crater today."

"You're going inside a volcano crater?" I asked. "Isn't that kind of dangerous?"

"Not usually," Jim said with a smile. "And I'll have on my space suit."

We all yelled good-bye to Jim. Then the Magic School Bus chugged off along Crater Rim Drive, one of the top sights in Volcanoes National Park. Our first stop was Sulfur Banks. We piled off the bus to check it out.

"Wait a minute, do you smell something funny?" Keesha asked.

"Yuck," Arnold said. "It smells like rotten eggs. Remember when we brought in eggs for our dinosaur project and forgot them over the weekend? That stunk!"

I looked over at Arnold. He was turning kind of green.

"According to my research," I said, "the smell of rotten eggs is caused by the sulfur gas they release. And this is called Sulfur Banks."

"Does that mean the volcano is full of rotten eggs?" Phoebe asked.

"No, it's just that rotten eggs and volcanoes both release sulfur gas," Ms. Frizzle explained. "But it smells just as bad!"

From the Desk of Ms. Frizzle

Smelly Sulfur: Rotten Eggs in Kilauea

Volcanic gas contains sulfur that eventually cools and turns into crystals. These spiky sulfur crystals can sometimes be seen close to volcanic vents. When water vapor condenses around them, they can really smell! The smell comes from the rotten-egg odor of sulfur.

I guess Arnold couldn't take it anymore. "Last one in the bus is a rotten egg!" he yelled. And we all made a run for it!

Ms. Frizzle started up the bus and announced, "Next stop, Thurston Lava Tube."

"Wow, I wish I had brought my skateboard," Carlos said. "How tubular would it be to ride a lava tube?"

The bus pulled up beside the sign for the

lava tube. We all crowded around to read it. Ralphie had done his report on lava tubes, so he helped explain it.

I wanted to be the first to explore the lava tube, so I made a run for the entrance. It was kind of spooky inside. I could see where the fiery lava had rushed through. And there were lava icicles dripping from the ceiling.

"Look out, D.A.," Carlos screamed behind me. "Some lava is coming through again!"

I ran through that lava tube like my life depended on it! I could almost feel the hot lava rushing in behind me. I made it out just in time.

Only problem was, Carlos had pulled one of his practical jokes on me! He came walking out of the lava tube with a big grin on his face.

"Gee, D.A., I didn't really think you'd fall for that," he said.

"Do you really think I believed you?" I said, trying to sound cool. "I was just practicing my sprinting."

What Is a Lava Tube?

by Ralphie

What is a lava tube? It's a big empty tube formed when a layer of lava cools and hardens while hot lava is still flowing underneath it. The hardened lava forms a roof over the "tube" of hot lava. As the level of flowing lava in the tube starts to drop, hot lava drips off the roof, creating formations that look like lava icicles!

When the lava inside the tube stops flowing, a big empty tube is left – like the Thurston Lava Tube.

tube of hot lava

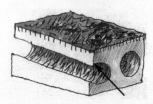

lava tube

Just then, I spied a sign not far away. It was sitting right in the middle of a lava field. And that lava looked smooth and flat!

I glanced over at Tim. He had just caught sight of the same sign. I took off like a streak of lightning toward it, pulling my buzzer out of my backpack as I ran.

Soon, I heard footsteps pounding behind me. I threw a look over my shoulder. Tim was gaining on me. I grabbed the buzzer tighter in my hand and ran even faster! Tim raced up beside me just as I started to read.

Blaaahhht! Blaaahhht!

"*Pahoehoe!*" we both screamed.

Ms. Frizzle and the rest of the kids came running up. "Pa-what?" Ms. Frizzle asked.

"Pahoehoe!" we yelled again.

"Correct!" the Friz said. "You're still in a wonderful tie!"

I couldn't believe it, either. Would we ever break this tie?

"Are you ready for the next tiebreaker question?" the Friz asked, pulling a question out of her shirt pocket.

Two Kinds of Lava

The two types of lava get their names from Hawaiian words.

Aa lava is pronounced *ah-ah*. It is thick, jagged, and fast moving. It carries sharp chunks of lava called *scoria*. A flow of aa lava flattens most things in its path and can be 220 feet (67 m) thick!

Pahoehoe lava is pronounced *pa-hoy-hoy*. It is more smooth on its surface and fluid and sometimes contains more gas than aa lava. Pahoehoe lava forms ropy patterns as it cools. A flow of pahoehoe lava is thinner than aa lava. Pahoehoe lava usually flows around trees and other obstacles and is only about three feet (1 m) thick.

"Oh, come on," Arnold interrupted, looking at me and Tim. "Can't we just call it a tie?"

"No way!" I yelled.

"Way no way!" Tim added.

"Give us the next question, Ms. Frizzle," I said, still panting for breath.

"What is the name of the new island being formed by underwater volcanic activity south of Hawaii?"

No buzzers buzzed. I looked nervously at Tim. He looked as clueless as I did.

"Ms. Frizzle, who would know something like that?" he said. Then he gave me a nervous glance.

"Not me," I admitted. "But I'll find out!"

"Hey, where's Carlos?" Phoebe said. "I think I saw him wandering off across the lava field."

Just then we all heard a scream echo across the lava field.

"Ouch, ouch!" Carlos was yelling.

We all took off running to find out what was wrong. As we got closer to Carlos, we saw him trying to move his feet. The soles of his shoes had melted by walking across a hot lava surface. Now Carlos was back on the cooler lava — but his feet were stuck!

"Help!" Carlos yelled when he saw us. "I'm stuck!"

CHAPTER 4

"Ms. Frizzle," I called out. "We've got to do something!"

I turned around to see where the Friz was. Then I saw a big yellow copter flying toward us. It was the Magic School Helicopter to the rescue!

The Friz flew the copter over to where Carlos was struggling in the lava. She hovered above him and then lowered down a rescue rope ladder.

"Carlos," she yelled over the sound of the rotor. "Untie your shoes — they're history!"

We all watched as Carlos reached down and untied the laces of his favorite sneakers.

40

Then he stretched up and grabbed hold of the rope ladder.

"You can do it, Carlos!" Keesha yelled.

Carlos pulled his feet out of his sneakers as he climbed up the ladder into the copter.

"You're lucky that lava was cooling, Carlos," Ms. Frizzle said. "Fresh lava can be as hot as a furnace."

"Ah, that stuff wasn't so hot," Carlos said, trying to regain his cool. "It was just like being stuck in a bunch of bubble gum."

"Well, from now on," Ms. Frizzle warned, "try to stay out of sticky situations, Carlos."

"Just think," I said. "Carlos's sneakers are now part of the state of Hawaii."

"We're lucky *Carlos* isn't part of the state of Hawaii!" Arnold said.

The Friz flew the helicopter over to safe ground and landed it.

"Come on, everybody," she yelled. "Let's see Kilauea from the air!"

We all piled inside the Magic School Helicopter and strapped on our seat belts. Carlos was fanning his feet to get them to cool off.

"That was a sticky situation," he said.

"I think you lost your cool, Carlos," Phoebe said.

Ms. Frizzle revved up the engine of the helicopter and we rose straight up into the air. Soon we were soaring above the lava fields.

"Look," Ralphie said. "You can see the red lava flowing down the side of the volcano!"

"They call it a river of fire," I said, remembering the research I had done.

Rivers of Fire
by D.A.

At times, Hawaiian lava flows are so steady that they look like rivers of fire! The molten rock moves in a thin stream down the volcanic mountain. It glows red-hot until it slowly spreads out and cools down. Other times a cool crust forms on the lava, forcing the river of fire into an underground lava tube.

"Why doesn't the lava blast out of Kilauea?" Ralphie asked. "I thought all volcanoes blew their tops."

We all looked down at the lava pumping out of Kilauea. It was fiery red, but it looked more like a quiet stream than an explosive blast.

"Not all volcanoes erupt in the same way," Ms. Frizzle explained. "And Kilauea is a great example of the Hawaiian type — slow but steady."

From the Desk of Ms. Frizzle

Spectacular Strombolians, Violent Vulcanians, Hot Hawaiians, and Phenomenal Plinians!

Volcanoes erupt in different ways — from steady to spectacular!

Hawaiian eruptions are quiet and slow. Thin, liquid lava flows out in slow, steady, red-hot streams.

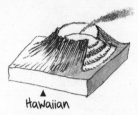

Hawaiian

Strombolian eruptions are wild and dramatic. Thick lava explodes out in separate bursts. There are loud explosions as the lava shoots into the air.

Strombolian

Vulcanian

Vulcanian eruptions are full of large lava blocks and lava bombs. The more pasty lava plugs up the volcano's opening, causing pressure to build in the volcano. When it blows, lava, gas, rocks, and dust shoot high and far into the air.

▲
Plinian

Plinian eruptions are the wildest of all. Huge blocks of thick lava explode from the top or sides of the volcano, forming fine ash. This cloud of ash reaches up more than 15 miles (25 km) above the earth. Sometimes a burning cloud of gas and ash blasts out and races down the volcano at speeds of up to 150 miles per hour (241 km/hr)!

"I sure am glad we're visiting a volcano in Hawaii," Carlos said. "Or I might be part of a lava field right now."

"Ms. Frizzle," Arnold said, "what's the big hole in that mountaintop? We're not going to do anything stupid, like fly inside, are we?"

"You can relax, Arnold," the Friz said. "We're just taking in the sights. That big volcano you see is Mauna Loa. It's the largest volcano in the world. It's so big that Kilauea just sits on its shoulder."

Mauna Loa was awesome! We flew over its crater, which looked like the surface of some faraway planet.

"Where do you think Jim is?" I asked. "He could be making a scientific discovery this very minute."

"Let's go check it out," the Friz said. "Kilauea, here we come!" She banked the helicopter right over Mauna Loa and headed back toward Kilauea.

On the way, Keesha pulled out a drawing pad from her backpack. She drew a volcano for us and we all added information about what was inside.

Inside a Volcano

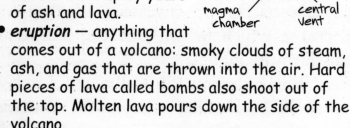

- **crater** — the opening at the top of a volcano. Lava, ash, gas, and steam explode out of it.
- **cone** — the sides of the volcano built up by years of ash and lava.
- **eruption** — anything that comes out of a volcano: smoky clouds of steam, ash, and gas that are thrown into the air. Hard pieces of lava called bombs also shoot out of the top. Molten lava pours down the side of the volcano.
- **central vent** — the vent that lets magma rise from the magma chamber to the surface.
- **side vent** — a vent branching off from the central vent. Pressure pushes magma through the side vent and out the side of the volcano.
- **magma chamber** — the place where molten magma gathers after it travels up from the earth's mantle. Gas pressure forces magma from the chamber into vents toward the surface.

I started to think about how cool it was to be a volcanologist like Jim. You could be so close to nature in action — it would almost be like taking a journey to the center of the earth! Now I had yet another career to consider. How would I ever choose between being a paleontologist, a microbiologist, a zoologist, or a volcanologist? So much science, so little time!

Carlos interrupted my thoughts. "Hey, I'll bet that's Jim right there," he yelled and pointed down into the Kilauea crater.

I looked out the window and saw a small white figure below us. It looked like an astronaut on the moon!

"Yep, that must be him," I said. "He has on his spaced-out suit."

We flew over where Jim was busy taking measurements of the air quality inside the crater. I remembered that volcanoes release a lot of gas, some of it poisonous. When Jim heard our big yellow copter, he looked up and waved.

From Jim's Volcanologist Files

Too Hot to Handle: Tools of the Trade

suit — a full-body covering with a metal coating that keeps out intense heat.

level — a tool to measure small changes in ground level that foretell an eruption.

gloves — made of heat-resistant asbestos to gather samples of warm magma.

thermometer — used to take temperatures of hot lava.

gas bottle — used to collect samples of volcanic gas

binoculars, tape measures, compass, two-way radio — tools to help a volcanologist take measurements and survive!

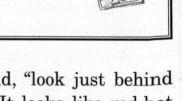

"Wow," Ralphie said, "look just behind where Jim is standing. It looks like red-hot lava."

We all saw what Ralphie was talking about, because suddenly red-hot lava started spurting up into the air in a fountain of fire.

Jim didn't even have time to turn around to see what was happening. He was knocked to the ground by the heat, or maybe a flying piece of lava!

"Ms. Frizzle," I yelled. "We've got to save him!"

I didn't have to tell the Friz to swing into action. She was already swinging the helicopter around and zooming down toward Jim. As the copter descended into the volcano crater, Jim waved his arms at us.

"We've got to land," Ms. Frizzle said. "He can't make it out of here by himself."

The Friz brought the copter to rest a few yards away from Jim. We all watched as he began to inch his way toward the copter. I could tell the Friz wanted to run out and help him. But she didn't have on any protective gear — and that lava spray looked as red-hot as the Friz's hair!

Finally, Jim reached us. The Friz threw open the passenger door and pulled him in. We all felt the heat of the volcano rush in like an oven door was just opened. As soon as Jim was safely inside, we slammed the door closed and took off.

"Whew, that was a close one," Jim said as he took off the top of his volcanologist suit.

"Ms. Frizzle," Arnold said. "Can we get out of here? I think I've learned my lesson about real lava. It's not made from vinegar and baking soda!"

With a grin, the Friz lifted the copter up out of the Kilauea crater. This was turning out to be one field trip that was too hot to handle!

CHAPTER 5

After our close call in the crater, the Friz decided we all needed to cool off for a while. She asked Jim to come along with us for a trip to the beach. He brought along snorkeling gear for everybody.

"Look out at the water," he said. "What do you see?"

"Water," Arnold said.

"Right," Jim said with a grin. "But underneath the water is a whole other world. Put on your snorkels and face masks and follow me."

Soon we were all floating on our stomachs with our heads down in the water. The snorkels let us breathe while our faces were underwater.

Jim was right. It was a whole other world! We could see hundreds of beautiful fish swimming below us. They were striped and spotted, in every color and every shape. The ocean floor was covered with beautiful and strange coral formations. I decided right then and there that I was going to be an oceanographer when I grew up. That's someone who studies the amazing world of the oceans.

Suddenly, we saw a long green shape move toward us in the water. As soon as Jim spotted it, he motioned to us and started swimming to the shore. I didn't waste any time . . . because I knew what was coming might be a moray eel — six feet of gross fish.

"What was that?" Arnold asked as we climbed out of the water and took off our snorkeling gear.

"Arnold, it's better that you don't know," Ralphie said, smiling.

Then Ms. Frizzle said, "Let's get inside the Magic School Bus. There's something I want to show you."

We weren't sure what the Friz had in mind, but we all climbed on board. Jim sat beside me in the seat in front, right behind Ms. Frizzle. I thought about what he did for a living and decided that I wanted to be a volcanologist again, rather than an oceanographer. It seems like everything I want to be ends with *-ographer* or *-ologist*!

Ms. Frizzle started up the Magic School Bus and motored on down the beach. Then suddenly, she made a hard left turn, straight into the ocean!

"Stop!" Arnold screamed as the Magic School Bus dove into a huge wave. The water level started to rise around our windows, and fish came up and pressed their faces against the glass to see us.

"Ms. Frizzle, do you know what you're doing?" I asked nervously.

"Don't worry, D.A.," the Friz said. "I have it all under control."

A second later, she pressed a red button on the control panel that had a picture of a submarine on it.

Whew! Not a minute too soon, the Magic School Bus turned into the Magic School Sub. Soon we were floating out into the deep ocean. Just as we caught our breath, the Friz turned the nose of the sub downward.

"Where are we going?" Carlos yelled.

"We're heading down to see where the earth is forming a new seafloor," the Friz said.

"A new floor?" Arnold said with a squeal. "How does that happen?"

"I know," Tim said. "She's talking about tectonic plates."

"What are plates doing on the ocean floor?" Carlos asked. "Do the fish eat off them?"

"Let me explain," Tim said. He read his report to us.

Trembling Tectonic Plates
by Tim

Why do some parts of the world have more volcanoes than others? The earth's surface was separated into large pieces of land called tectonic plates. Forces deep within the earth cause these plates to shift, grind against each other, and move apart. Magma from the earth's core squeezes through the cracks created by shifting plates. Then, boom! There's a volcano.

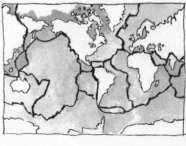

Wow. I was impressed by Tim's explanation. Now I was really worried about winning the quiz bowl!

"Look, kids," Jim said. "There's a black smoker! That means we're close to underwater volcanic activity."

"Hey, I know about that," I burst in, eager to show Jim how much I knew about volcanoes. I read my report aloud.

Burning Black Smokers
by D.A.

Smokers are really hot underwater springs. They pop up where the ocean floor is spreading apart along midocean ridges, and other places where tectonic plates come together. Smokers spew out hot, acidic, black water full of metals like copper, lead, and zinc.

"Dynamite explanation, Dorothy Ann," Jim said. I threw a glance over at Tim to see if he was impressed. But he was busy reading a book about underwater volcanic activity near the Hawaiian Islands.

"Oh, my gosh!" I said aloud. I had almost forgotten about the tiebreaker question: What island is being formed by volcanic activity right now?

I ran over to the bookshelf on the sub walls and pulled down a book about underwater volcanoes. I started to speed-read like crazy. I couldn't let Tim beat me like this!

Suddenly, I saw Tim jump up and run to his backpack. I just knew he had found the answer, but he couldn't find his buzzer! I kept reading — faster and faster! Just in time, I found it. I grabbed my buzzer and pressed it.

Blaahhht! Blaaahht!

"Not again!" I yelled.

Ms. Frizzle asked us to say our answers at the count of three. One. Two. Three.

"Loihi!" we both said.

"Another tie!" the Friz said. "Isn't this exciting, class?"

"You bet it is," I said. "And my team is going to win."

"I'll believe that when I see it," Tim said smugly.

"Okay, then, listen up," Ms. Frizzle announced. "Here is the next tiebreaker question: How long does it take for molten lava to harden?"

"What!" I said. "Who would know that?"

"Ridiculous," Tim added. "How could we ever find that out?"

Then Tim and I both grabbed for more research books to see if we could find the answer. As Ms. Frizzle guided the sub across the ocean floor, Jim talked to the rest of the kids about underwater volcanoes. I listened with one ear while I tried to read about how fast lava hardens.

"So why are there so many hot spots around here?" Wanda asked. "The water out there looks cold."

Fire Down Below: Secrets of Underwater Volcanoes

Scientists believe that there may be more volcanoes underwater than on land! The most common type of underwater volcanoes are called rift volcanoes. They form when two plates are continuously pulled apart at speeds of up to about 1 inch (2.5 cm) per year. Magma oozes up between these plates, and volcanoes are formed.

Rift volcanoes are forming under the Atlantic Ocean right now. They are making the Atlantic grow one half inch (1.3 cm) wider per year!

"The water *is* cold," Jim explained. "But under the ocean floor, hot lava is bubbling away, trying to get out. That's why this area of the world is called the Ring of Fire."

"That sounds scary," Wanda said.

"Especially if you live on a little island near a volcanic eruption," Tim added.

"Maybe it's scary if you're in a little yellow submarine, too," said Arnold in a quiet voice.

From the Desk of Ms. Frizzle

The Ring of Fire

Ring of Fire

The Ring of Fire circles the edges of the continents and islands around the Pacific Ocean. It contains 500 or more active volcanoes!

Some eruptions in the Ring of Fire have been incredibly violent and killed many people.

Other eruptions are quiet and have slow lava flows, like many of the ones in Hawaii.

"Don't worry, Arnold," I said. "I'm sure Ms. Frizzle wouldn't take us anywhere near the Ring of Fire."

Just then, there was a rumble from the seafloor below us.

"Uh, I don't know about that," Jim said. "I think we may have wandered near some hot spots."

A louder rumble spread across the ocean floor and shook the windows of the sub. We all looked at one another with wide eyes.

Then there was a loud *BOOM*.

And the Magic School Sub began to bounce around in the water like a yellow rubber duck!

CHAPTER 6

"Ms. Frizzle," I yelled, "you've got to do something!"

I was hanging on to the sides of the Magic School Sub to keep from sliding across the floor. The rest of the kids were holding on to anything that seemed solid. Everybody was screaming.

"Yikes! This is worse than that ride we took through a tornado!" Wanda said.

"It's even worse than traveling back to the Jurassic Age," Ralphie yelled. "I think we're goners!"

"Don't say that," I cried. "I still need a chance to win the quiz bowl!"

Jim was hanging on to part of the sub's control panel, where the Friz was desperately trying to get us away from the volcano's eruption. It didn't seem to be working!

"I don't think we can outrun this, Ms. Frizzle," Jim said. "An underwater eruption is pretty wild. We'd better just hold on tight and try to ride it out!"

From Jim's Volcanologist Files

There She Blows! Underwater Eruptions

During a shallow underwater eruption, incredibly hot magma hits cold water. This makes the water turn into steam, which makes it expand. A huge amount of pressure is built up. That makes for loud explosions and huge clouds of steam!

All of a sudden, the rumbling beneath us got louder. It reminded me of what I had read about Krakatoa, another volcano in the Ring of Fire. Only I hoped we weren't in for that big of a boom!

"Jim, what's that noise?" I called.

Krakatoa – the Volcano Heard Halfway around the World
by D.A.

Krakatoa is a small volcanic island in the South Pacific. In 1883, the island made an earsplitting eruption! It was so loud that people more than 3,000 miles (4,828 km) away heard the roar. For the next two years, volcanic dust filled the air in places as far away as London, England!

"It sounds like a major vent is blowing," Jim answered, trying to sound calm. But this was way too hot for even a volcanologist to handle!

All of a sudden, the Magic School Sub seemed to go airborne! We squirted up out of the water on a plume of steam. And outside the window we saw blue sky instead of blue water.

But it didn't stay blue for long. Soon there was volcanic ash floating around everywhere.

It was awesome! I wished I had my camera. Here we were in the middle of a volcanic eruption, and I had no way of recording it!

"Whoa!" Carlos yelled. "I think somebody just hit the down button."

Carlos was right. Suddenly, we started to fall out of the sky like a brick. Submarines — even Magic School Submarines — just don't fly!

KERSPLASH! We hit the water with a smack and bobbed up and down for a while. Ms. Frizzle was busy at the controls, trying to figure out how to get the sub in reverse and away from the volcano.

That's when I looked out the sub window. The tip of a new volcanic island was sticking up above the ocean surface. And red-hot lava was belching out of its mouth.

From Jim's Volcanologist Files

The Tip of the Volcano

New islands pop up in the Pacific Ocean because of underwater volcanic activity. The Hawaiian Islands are only the tips of an enormous undersea mountain range that rests on top of a hot spot in the earth's mantle.

"Ms. Frizzle," I yelled. "Throw it in reverse — fast!"

The Friz was fast, but not fast enough. Just as the Magic School Sub started to shoot backward, a fiery spray of lava splattered down on top of us. It turned the sub on its end, with its nose sticking up into the air. Then the lava settled all around us. And everything went black outside!

"What will we do?" Arnold cried. "When that lava hardens, we'll be part of a volcano — forever!"

"D.A. and Tim," Carlos said, "you better figure out the tiebreaker question — quick!"

CHAPTER 7

I looked at my watch. According to my calculations, the lava had hit our sub just about one minute ago. Already I could see that it was losing its reddish glow. How long would it be before it turned hard as a rock?

Tim came up to stand beside me and watch the lava harden.

"You know something, D.A.?" he said. "I don't really care about getting that tiebreaker question right. I don't even care about winning the quiz bowl anymore. I just want to get out of here and go home!"

I took one last look at the lava. It no

longer looked soft and oozy. It wasn't hard yet, but it was beginning to set like cement. I checked my watch. Four minutes had passed.

Then I looked around the sub at Tim, Carlos, Wanda, Phoebe, Keesha, Ralphie, and Arnold. And suddenly, I didn't care about winning the quiz bowl, either. All that was important was getting home — and not spending the rest of our lives in a volcano!

"Ms. Frizzle," I called out. "I have a plan!"

I ran over to the sub controls and told the Friz my idea. Her red hair seemed to spring up with excitement as she listened. Then she started punching the buttons on the control panel. Finally, she found the one we needed.

Above our heads, we heard the start of a loud grinding sound.

"Ms. Frizzle, what's going on?" Arnold asked hopefully.

"It's the Magic School Drill," the Friz said, with a twinkle in her eye. "And it sounds

as though it's doing a great job of cutting through that lava!"

As the drill worked its way through the lava, it pulled the Magic School Sub up toward the surface of the volcano. And, all of a sudden, we could see light through the windows of the sub!

"Hurray!" we yelled.

"Whew!" the Friz said, wiping the sweat off her forehead. "That was a *hard* situation to get out of!"

Without missing a beat, the Friz punched in a few more buttons on the control panel. The drill at the front of the sub turned into a helicopter rotor. And seconds later, the Magic School Sub was transformed into the Magic School Helicopter.

Everyone cheered as our helicopter soared safely up above the new volcanic island.

Things looked pretty strange up there in the sky. Ms. Frizzle explained that's because volcanoes can affect the weather in dramatic ways.

From the Desk of Ms. Frizzle

Weather Report:
Downpour of Volcanic Ash

Volcanic eruptions change the weather and the environment. After an eruption, there can be months of strong winds, heavy rains, and mudflows. During large, explosive eruptions, lightning can sometimes be seen flashing inside and around the rising column of ash.

Volcanic eruptions can also create spectacular sunrises and sunsets because of the gas and ash thrown into the stratosphere. After Krakatoa erupted, people in Sri Lanka reported that the sun looked green. On the other side of the world, in Trinidad, the sun appeared blue!

We flew over the blue water of the Pacific, back toward the Hawaiian Islands. Down below, we spotted a pretty green island.

"Ms. Frizzle," Arnold asked weakly. "Could we touch down on that island for a while? I feel airsick and seasick. I just want to feel my feet on land."

"That might not be such a good idea, Arnold," said Jim. "We don't want to be in the area if a tsunami comes."

Super Tsunamis – Scary Surfs!
by D.A.

Tsunamis (soo-nah-me) are huge tidal waves caused by landslides or earthquakes. Volcanoes can also cause small tsunamis. Tsunami is a Japanese word meaning "wave breaking in the harbor." After the Krakatoa eruption, more than 36,000 people died from drowning in the huge black wall of water that washed over Pacific islands.

"Tsunami? What's that?" asked Phoebe.

"I know!" I shouted. "According to my research, volcanic eruptions can cause giant waves."

Arnold looked a little queasy. "Um, maybe we shouldn't stop at that island after all, Ms. Frizzle. Maybe we should just go home."

"Stupendous idea, Arnold!" said the Friz. "We'll drop you off at the park, Jim, and then I think it's time the Magic School Bus heads home."

Everyone in the Magic School Copter broke into cheers. I settled back into my seat with a sigh of relief. Maybe I'd grow up to be a volcanologist like Jim someday. But for now, I was ready to say *aloha* to Hawaii and *hello* to home!

CHAPTER 8

I walked into Ms. Frizzle's classroom with my research in hand. It had taken a lot of work, but I had found an answer to the tiebreaker question. I was ready to make a report to the class.

"Where's Ms. Frizzle?" I asked, looking around the room. "I found out how long it takes for lava to harden."

"Dorothy Ann, the quiz bowl is over," Tim interrupted. "You know Ms. Frizzle declared it a tie. And we're all winners because we aren't stuck inside that volcano anymore!"

"This isn't about the quiz bowl, Tim," I said patiently. "It's about science."

"But I don't want to know how long it takes for lava to harden," Arnold said. "I don't even want to think about it!"

I looked around the classroom at everyone's faces. Nobody seemed to want to know how long it takes for lava to harden. I was ready to bet that none of them would be an *-ologist* when they grew up!

With a sigh, I tacked my report to the wall. That way, anyone with a *real* interest in science could read it.

Behind me, I heard Carlos say to Arnold, "This time, you can pour in the vinegar, Arnold. But be ready to duck — fast!"

Hard as Rock!
by D.A.

When lava explodes from a volcano, it is red-hot liquid. As soon as it hits the outside air, it starts to cool.

Lava that flows over land cools by radiating out its heat. The lava on top of a flow cools off first because the air takes away its heat faster than from the lava underneath. Within a few minutes, a crust forms on the lava's surface. Later, the lava under the crust slowly cools and hardens.

Lava that hits cold ocean water cools much faster. It cools so fast that it "freezes" into a black glass and shatters to pieces.

Hot lava that hits cold ocean water creates an explosion called a tephra jet. This is a cloud of steam, hot water, and tephra (tiny, glassy fragments of lava).

If you get caught in a lava flow get out as as fast as you can . . . because cold lava turns as hard as rock!

MAUNA LOA
HAWAII

I turned around to see what was happening. Arnold was standing in back of his rebuilt model volcano. He was holding the plastic bottle full of vinegar. Carlos was standing nearby with a big grin on his face.

"Ready for the eruption, everybody?" Arnold asked. Then he began to pour the vinegar into the mouth of the volcano.

There was a bubbling sound. Then it grew louder. Suddenly, a blast of red lava came blowing out of the volcano! It splattered all over Arnold and Carlos. It even hit my lava report!

"We did it! We did it!" Carlos yelled happily.

Just then, Ms. Frizzle walked into the classroom. Her mouth fell open when she saw the volcano erupting.

"Congratulations, Arnold and Carlos," she said with a smile. "That's the first Strombolian eruption I've ever seen from a model volcano. You kids are really hot stuff!"

Volcano Quiz Bowl

1. What is the most active volcano on Earth?
2. What are the two types of lava?
3. What is a volcanologist?
4. What are the four types of volcanic eruptions?
5. What are tectonic plates?
6. What are black smokers?
7. What is the Ring of Fire?
8. What is the difference between magma and lava?
9. What is Hawaii's youngest volcano?
10. What was the volcano whose eruption was heard around the world?
11. What are rift volcanoes?
12. How do volcanoes change the weather?
13. What is a tsunami?
14. What is sulfur?
15. What is a lava tube?
16. What is Mount Saint Helens?
17. Where is the farthest away that volcanoes have been found?

18. What is a hot spot?
19. What are black sand beaches?
20. What larger volcano does Kilauea rest on?

Answer Key:

1. Kilauea
2. aa and pahoehoe
3. A scientist who studies volcanoes
4. Strombolian, Vulcanian, Hawaiian, and Plinian
5. Tectonic plates are plates that make up the outer shell of the earth, which includes its crust. When they shift and move apart, they create volcanoes and earthquakes.
6. Black smokers are underwater hot springs.
7. The Ring of Fire is an area around the Pacific Ocean that has 500 active volcanoes.
8. Magma is molten rock from the earth's core. Magma becomes lava when it hits the earth's surface.
9. Loihi, an underwater volcano growing on the southern part of the Hawaiian Islands
10. Krakatoa was heard on different continents when it exploded.

11. Ocean rift volcanoes are volcanoes that are underwater.
12. After a volcanic eruption, there are strong winds, heavy rainfall, and clouds of sulfur that stop sunlight from hitting the earth.
13. A tsunami is a powerful tidal wave created by the force of landslides or earthquakes. It can wipe out coastal villages and kill thousands of people.
14. Sulfur is the smelly gas belched out by erupting volcanoes.
15. A lava tube occurs when the top of a lava flow hardens but there remains a flow of lava underneath the hardened lava roof. After this drains away, a tube is left behind.
16. Mount Saint Helens is a volcano in Washington State. It erupted in 1980 for the first time since 1857.
17. There are volcanoes in outer space.
18. Hot spots are places where magma rises from the earth's interior through tectonic plates to create volcanoes.

19. Black sand beaches are created when hot lava meets the cool ocean.
20. Kilauea rests on the side of the larger volcano Mauna Loa.

Join my class on all of our Magic School Bus adventures!

The Truth about Bats
The Search for the Missing Bones
The Wild Whale Watch
Space Explorers
Twister Trouble
The Giant Germ
The Great Shark Escape
Penguin Puzzle
Dinosaur Detectives
Expedition Down Under
Insect Invaders
Amazing Magnetism
Polar Bear Patrol
Electric Storm
Voyage to the Volcano
Butterfly Battle
Food Chain Frenzy